D1261950

Children of the World

Mexico

For their help in the preparation of *Children of the World: Mexico*, the editors gratefully thank Nicolas Escalante, Embassy of Mexico (Canada), Ottawa; William Jarrett, the Center for Latin America, University of Wisconsin-Milwaukee; Gloria Jimenez and Filiberto Murguia, the Spanish Center, Milwaukee; Armando Rios, Milwaukee, Wis.; Rita Tenorio, the Milwaukee Public Schools; and Carlos Tujalte, Embassy of Mexico (U.S.), Washington, D.C.

Library of Congress Cataloging-in-Publication Data

Ikuhara, Yoshiyuki, 1947-
  Mexico.

  (Children of the world)
  Bibliography: p.
  Includes index.
  Summary: Presents the life of a girl and her family
in Guadalajara, Mexico's second largest city,
describing her home and school activities and the
festivals, religious ceremonies, and national holidays
of her country.
  1. Mexico — Social life and customs — Juvenile
literature. 2. Children — Mexico — Juvenile literature.
[1. Mexico — Social life and customs. 2. Family life —
Mexico] I. Knowlton, MaryLee, 1946-
II. Sachner, Mark, 1948- . III. Title.
IV. Series: Children of the world (Milwaukee, Wis.)
F1210.I48   1987   972   86-42800
ISBN 1-55532-186-0
ISBN 1-55532-161-5 (lib. bdg.)

North American edition first published in 1987 by

Gareth Stevens, Inc.
7221 West Green Tree Road   Milwaukee, Wisconsin 53223, USA

This work was originally published in shortened form consisting of Section I only.

Typeset by Ries Graphics ltd., Milwaukee.
Design: Laurie Shock & Gary Moseley.
Map design: Gary Moseley.

1 2 3 4 5 6 7 8 9 92 91 90 89 88 87

Children of the World
Mexico

Photography by
Yoshiyuki Ikuhara

Edited by
MaryLee Knowlton &
Mark J. Sachner

Gareth Stevens Publishing
Milwaukee

... a note about *Children of the World*:

The children of the world live in fishing towns and urban centers, on islands and in mountain valleys, on sheep ranches and fruit farms. This series follows one child in each country through the pattern of his or her life. Candid photographs show the children with their families, at school, at play, and in their communities. The text describes the dreams of the children and, often through their own words, tells how they see themselves and their lives.

Each book also explores events that are unique to the country in which the child lives, including festivals, religious ceremonies, and national holidays. The *Children of the World* series does more than tell about foreign countries. It introduces the children of each country and shows readers what it is like to be a child in that country.

... and about *Mexico*:

Maria Elena lives in Guadalajara, Mexico's second largest city, with her parents and two young sisters. Her family's modest success allows her to enjoy the diversity of life in a city both ancient and modern. Elena's many interests keep her busy from morning till night at school, in the markets, and at a variety of festivals and celebrations.

To enhance this book's value in libraries and classrooms, comprehensive reference sections include up-to-date data about Mexico's geography, demographics, language, currency, education, culture, industry, and natural resources. *Mexico* also features a bibliography, research topics, activity projects, and discussions of such subjects as Mexico City, the country's history, political system, ethnic and religious composition, and immigrants to Canada and the U.S.

The living conditions and experiences of children in Mexico vary tremendously according to economic, environmental, and ethnic situations. The reference sections help bring to life for young readers the diversity and richness of the culture and heritage of Mexico.

CONTENTS

LIVING IN MEXICO: Maria Elena,
a Girl from the City

¡Hola! yo soy María Elena Manzo Rios

"Hello! I'm Maria Elena Manzo Rios."

Elena is a ten-year-old girl from Mexico, the land of the sun. She lives with her father, Francisco; her mother, also named Elena; and her two sisters, five-year-old Cristina and three-year-old Isabel. They are a Roman Catholic family. More than 95% of all Mexicans are Catholic.

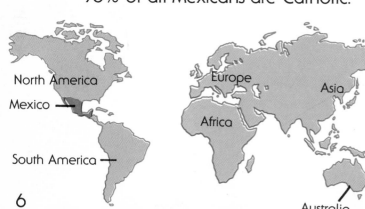

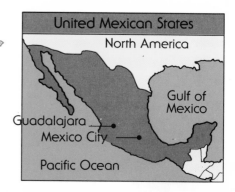

"My doll Rosita was a present from *Mamá Grande,* my grandmother."

Guadalajara, Elena's Home Town

Elena and her family live in Guadalajara, the second largest city in Mexico. It is also the capital of the state of Jalisco. The city was built in 1542 by the Spanish. Today it is home to more than 3 million people.

Guadalajara is a lively mixture of both old and new. As a major Mexican city, it is a center of business and industry. However, many historical buildings, such as the Cathedral and its four surrounding plazas, the Degollado Theater, and the Basilica de Zapopan, remain from its earliest days when Spain ruled the country.

Basilica de Zapopan. Worshippers kneel on the stone pavement to pray.

Colorful Christmas decorations stay up till after Epiphany.

8

Degollado Theater. Many plays and concerts are performed here.

Christmas decorations in Liberation Plaza.

In the northern part of the city is the Cabañas Orphanage, built in 1830. The mural by José Clement Orozco in the dome of its chapel is very famous. It is very high. To see it, you must either look straight up or use a mirror to reflect it.

Inside the Basilica de Zapopan. ►

The main street of Guadalajara is Juárez Avenue. Mexicans also call it the Avenue of September 16. September 16 is Mexican Independence Day. Parades are held along this avenue on Christmas and Independence Days.

In the center of the city is the Libertad Market. Here, about 4000 small shops sell everything from food and household goods to folk crafts. The famous Mexican pottery and glass are popular with foreign visitors.

Guadalajara is a long way from the sea and 5094 ft (1553 m) above sea level. During the rainy season of June and July, it rains for a while every day. For the rest of the year, the climate is very mild and pleasant.

Like Elena and her sisters, both their parents were born and raised in Guadalajara. They are of mixed Spanish and Indian heritage, or *mestizo*.

Juárez Avenue is the busiest street in Guadalajara.
There are no bus stops; the buses stop when people raise their hands.

A market in the center of Guadalajara.

Cooking and Eating

The staple food of the Mexican diet is the *tortilla,* a kind of crepe made of corn flour. The tortilla is like bread in our diet. When the tortilla is dried and fried in oil, it is called a *tostada.* Tortillas are eaten with soup, meat, or vegetables. When beans, tomatoes, chilies, avocados, and sometimes meat are added, a tortilla becomes a *taco!*

Elena's favorite food is *carne en su jugo,* a dish resembling a beef and onion soup. Her mother promises, "If you do well on the next sewing test, I will make carne soup and quesadillas." Elena loves *quesadillas.* Most of you would, too, because they are a lot like cheese pizza!

An endless variety of chilies, peas, and beans.

Tortilla, the staple food of Mexico.

Cactus and *guanges,* a type of pea.

Street vendors sell cooked food.

Some say there are 4000 types of traditional cooking in Mexico! Corn and beans have been grown here for thousands of years. But most people think of hot chili peppers when they think of Mexican food. Indeed, Mexico has many kinds of chilies. Chilies give a strong flavor to food, and they are full of vitamins. Elena's father loves chili sauce and pours it over most of his food.

Thanks to Guadalajara's mild climate, fruit grows in great quantities, and juices are sold on the street by vendors. In poor sections of the cities and villages, most food is sold by street vendors. Many customers cannot afford refrigerators. They must buy their food freshly picked or butchered each day.

The tap water is not good, so people buy bottled water for drinking and cooking. Every day trucks come with bottled water to sell.

16

A shop sign in Tlaquepaque.

Red glassware called *sangre de pichón* (pigeon blood).

Folk crafts.

Shopping in Tlaquepaque

Elena goes shopping with her mother to Tlaquepaque, about ten minutes by bus from home. Tlaquepaque is a shopping town. It is known for pottery, hand-blown glass, and many other kinds of handicrafts. Elena and her mother have come here to buy a birthday present for Elena's father.

Elena and her mother in Tlaquepaque.

Mariachi musicians.

Tlaquepaque is also known as the home of *mariachi* music. These strolling musicians are called *mariachis.* They are popular in larger cities like Guadalajara and Mexico City, as well as in tourist areas like Tlaquepaque.

The mariachis play many kinds of music. Elena's favorite songs are *corridos,* which are long, rhymed verses with witty words and simple tunes. Elena's mother tells her that she and Francisco used to come to Tlaquepaque when they were dating. Today Elena enjoys hearing the songs her parents have often told her about.

Elena's house. Workers are building a second story addition.

At Home with Elena's Family

Elena's home is in a new residential area twelve minutes by car from downtown Guadalajara. Nearby is an industrial area with many cement factories and oil refineries. Elena's parents bought this house nine years ago. It has three bedrooms, a living room, and a kitchen.

Most of the houses on the block have dogs, since there have been some robberies. Elena has a dog named Canelita, a gift from her grandmother.

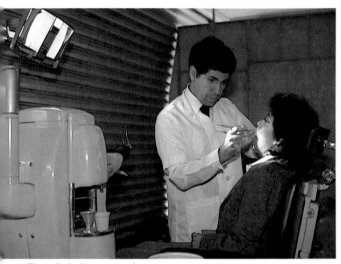

Elena's father at work.

Elena's father, Francisco, is a dentist. When he was just twelve, he began working as an assistant to a dentist. After graduating from dental school, he opened up a dental clinic in an area where many poorer people live.

Mexicans do not often go to the dentist even when they have a toothache, in part because so many of them are very poor. Elena's father provides low cost dental care to poor people.

Elena and her family have fun at home.

Elena's family eats all their meals together. Breakfast is at 7 a.m., and for Elena it is a very light meal, usually just milk and a cookie. After breakfast her father takes all the children to school on his way to work.

Lunch is the main meal of the day.

After school he brings them home for lunch, the main meal of the day. After lunch, people take a *siesta,* or nap. Most children don't sleep, but grown-ups do. After siesta, Francisco goes back to work. Elena washes dishes before she does her school homework. Cristina and Isabel play together, one moment quarreling and crying, and the next moment laughing together.

Dinner is the happiest time of the day for Elena. Although it is a very light meal, it is a time for families. Everyone talks about their day's events.

At supper everyone enjoys talking about the events of the day.

Elena loves to talk about her friends and her school. Often she tells stories she has made up to entertain Christina and Isabel. Her parents enjoy talking and listening to each other and their children at this peaceful time of the day.

The holiday begins with a church service.
The sermon seems longer than usual.

Mexico's Second Christmas

Today is January 6, the Feast of Epiphany (*Los Santos Reyes*). In Mexico children get presents at Epiphany in memory of the gifts presented by the Three Wise Men to the baby Jesus. It's like a second Christmas for the children of Mexico. The day begins with a church service in the morning.

Cutting the *rosca de reyes*.
Who will get the baby doll baked inside?

Blindfolded, Elena tries to break the piñata.

24

Elena and her father dance for their guests.

After church, the children of neighbors and relatives arrive for the festivities. A large pot called a *piñata* contains fruit and candy. The blindfolded children take turns trying to break the piñata with a stick. The piñata hangs on a string and swings back and forth, so it's not easy to break. Once it breaks everybody scrambles for the treats.

A high point of the party for Elena is dancing with her father. He has taught her all kinds of steps, and both of them are skilled dancers.

Elena helps her mother with the cleaning.

Working and Playing at Home

Elena has made three promises to her mother: to do things on her own, to look after her younger sisters, and to help her mother with housework. Since her sisters are still very little, they are not much help with the housework. Elena sometimes wishes she had older brothers or sisters to share the load and to play with.

Today Elena has done some cleaning and washing. She hangs out all the washing on the upstairs veranda. She will leave it there till it dries, rain or shine.

Hanging the clothes on the upstairs veranda.

Shopping at the supermarket.

The hardest promise to keep is to look after her sisters. They often do not obey her, and they cry if she gets angry with them. Then Elena gets scolded!

Being the oldest child can be very hard because it means having many responsibilities. But Elena's parents reward her for her help at home. They take her with them for special outings, and she feels that it all evens out.

Elena loves to read. Her favorite magazine is a weekly comic called "*Capulinita.*" She buys it with her allowance, her "*mi domingo,*" which is 100 *pesos* a week.

She also loves to read stories and fairy tales. She wants to write children's stories when she grows up. She writes her stories in a notebook and illustrates them with her own drawings. When she thinks she has a story just the way she wants it, she reads it to her sisters.

Elena will be in junior high school next September. To enter junior high, students must take an entrance examination. Elena has already begun studying for it.

All children must attend primary school. Most choose to go on to high school, but some do not. Some families are so poor that the children must go to work right after primary school. Other children get married very young. In Mexico, a boy can marry at sixteen and a girl at thirteen if they have their parents' permission.

Reading comics, an afterschool pleasure.

Watching TV after homework.

An illustrated story created by Elena.

Isabel wants someone to play with her.

Homework.

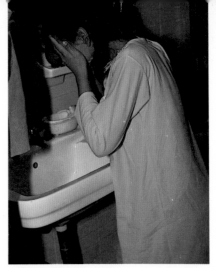

Elena washes before she goes to bed.
And she *always* brushes her teeth.

A slumber party with Lupe. Lots of giggling, not much sleeping.

Elena has a lot of school homework.
She knows she must study hard to
prepare for her writing career. When
school is out, she does her homework
before she does anything else. Then
she reads comics or watches TV. Her
favorite program is "My Clever Dog Joy,"
because the little dog reminds her of her own dog, Canelita.

Today Elena's cousin Lupe is coming to stay overnight. For fun,
all the children sleep in the same bed. They need only one
blanket over them, since even at night it is warm all year long.

Going to school.

Elena and Her Friends at School

In Mexico there is a big gap between the rich and the poor.
Elena's family is considered to be well-off. They can afford the
children's education as well as a TV set and two cars. Elena
knows she is very lucky. Her father's work among poorer
people has made her aware of other people's hardship.

Elena goes to Lucio Blanco Urbana School Número 49. The
building is 400 years old but has only been used as a school
since 1930. It is in the middle of town, and children commute
from all over the city.

The school classes are given in three sessions: 8 a.m. to 1
p.m., 2 p.m. to 6:30 p.m., and 7 p.m. to 9 p.m. The
evening session is for those over fifteen years old who did
not finish primary school when they were young. It has pupils
of all ages.

31

Textbooks.

Elena is ten years old and would normally be in the fifth grade. But she skipped a year in kindergarten, so she is in the sixth grade. Her class has 37 students. Students cannot go on to the next grade if they miss school often or if they don't pass their courses. So Elena's class has students from ten to fifteen years old.

The students all have to study the national language, Spanish, and mathematics, science, social studies, art, sewing, health, and physical education. They study two subjects a day. Since there are no school grounds or gym, they usually practice marching for ceremonies during physical education classes. Elena is good at Spanish and social studies, but not at sewing.

It's Friday, and an outdoor market is held in front of the school.

33

The school courtyard during recess.

Elena and her classmates.

Sewing class. Elena's improving!

Elena recites her homework for the class.

◄ One more hour till recess!

The teacher's son comes to school with her today.

Today Elena's teacher has brought her two-year-old son, José, to school. The girls take turns looking after him. The students are quite free, even during classtime. They talk to each other or even do knitting.

Mrs. Luze-Casillas, the principal.

The girls play with their dolls during recess.

The students salute the national flag.

The national flag ceremony.

During the class break, the girls play house and other games in the school courtyard. Some may not have eaten breakfast at home, and they catch up by munching bread.

The students practice once a month for the Independence Day and National Flag Day parades. The ceremonies have a different theme every month. This month the theme is "World Friendship." The lower grades wear the national costumes of different countries. The upper grades march and practice a flag-raising ceremony.

The children dress in the costumes of many nations to promote world friendship.

The lower grade boys dress up as cowboys.

School's Out!

After school the students all go home. Many students in Mexican schools are from poor families. They must get jobs when they are very young, so there are no school clubs or after school programs. Elena and her sisters go to her grandmother's house, and their father picks them up for lunch.

Elena plays a hopscotch game with the girls in her neighborhood. It is called "*bebeleche.*" The boys play soccer or play with their tops or marbles.

Usually boys and girls don't play together. Moral education at home is very strict, especially for girls. Boys dream of becoming *matadors,* bullfighters. Every girl looks forward to her fifteenth birthday when she wears a very special dress and is recognized as an adult.

Playing hopscotch.

Waiting for their father at Grandmother's house. Two of the little children are the brother and sister of Elena's father. Elena is older than her aunt and uncle.

At the supermarket.

Mexico is said to be the birthplace of cocoa. Elena loves many Mexican chocolate sweets, such as a chocolate layer cake called *Gansito* and a chocolate-coated jelly called *Submarino*.

The Wall Market changes locations every day. Every Wednesday it opens in front of Elena's house. People can buy everything from household goods and food to traditional Indian medicine. On other days Elena's family shops in a supermarket near their house. Many supermarket goods come from the United States.

Mexican candy.

The candy turns Elena's tongue red.

Walking home from the market.

Elena's had a long, full day, and she's tired.

Swimming with Lupe.

A Birthday Weekend

Every year Elena's family spends a weekend at the Guadalajara University Sports Club to celebrate her father's birthday. The club is like a resort hotel with all kinds of sports and games.

This year, because she has been so helpful at home, Elena gets to bring her cousin Lupe along. As soon as they arrive, Elena and Lupe change into bathing suits and jump into the pool. Living so far from the sea, the girls don't often get to swim. This is a treat they will talk about until next year.

In the evening the family throws a birthday party at the club. All their friends and relatives are there. Until the early hours of the morning they eat, drink, sing, and dance. The children get to stay up as long as they can stay awake.

Everybody dances at the birthday party!

Maria Elena says "¡Adios!" She hopes you will learn Spanish so
that someday you can read the books she is going to write.
"¡Hasta la vista!"

47

FOR YOUR INFORMATION: Mexico

Official name:
Estados Unidos Mexicanos
(es-TAH-dos u-NEE-dos meh-hee-CAN-os)

Capital:
Mexico City

United Mexican States

Many old ruins survive at Teotihuacán.

History

In ancient times Mexico was first a hunting and gathering society. It was then a farming society. The earliest villages appeared around 2000 B.C., or about 4000 years ago. The Spanish invaded Mexico in the sixteenth century. Up to that time, the history of Mexico is the history of the Indians.

Olmecs
About 2000 B.C. the Olmecs built a city near present-day Veracruz. Historical remains have been found in the ruins of La Venta. These remains include earthenware, clay figures, and huge stone sculptures of human faces.

Mexica
A large religious city appeared in the Central Plateau between 300 B.C. and 750 A.D. The city was named Teotihuacán. This means "City of the Gods." The largest remains of this city are near Mexico City. These remains include the Pyramid of the Sun. It is 215 ft (65½ m) high. Its volume is greater than any of the pyramids of Egypt.

Mayans

The Mayans originated in the jungles of Guatemala. In 100 B.C., they had a highly developed society in the Yucatán Peninsula. Hieroglyphic records of their rule survive. The Mayans developed a very accurate calendar. It shows only a 0.0002 day difference from the solar calendar calculated by modern astronomers. The Mayan civilization survived until 900 A.D.

Aztecs

The last great Indian empire was that of the Aztecs. It appeared about 1200 A.D. The Aztec capital was Tenochtitlán, at the site of the present Mexico City. Spain invaded 300 years later. At that time, Tenochtitlán was probably the largest city in the world. The Spaniards left records which tell of the great beauty and size of the city. After recording its beauty, they then destroyed most of it. The last remains of the floating flower gardens of the Aztec princes are in Xochimilco. Today Aztec boatmen pole tourists around the park's islands in flower-covered boats.

Colonial Period

In 1519 Hernán Cortés landed on the eastern shore of Mexico. With him were 315 Spanish soldiers. The Aztec Emperor Montezuma welcomed the light-skinned foreigners and treated them as honored guests.

Within two years of their landing, the Spanish had betrayed the Aztecs. They took over the government and destroyed the city. The land was given to Spanish governors. They built huge estates or farms, which they ran with Indian slave labor. These estates were called *haciendas*. The Catholic Church and the Spanish government shared the great wealth from Mexico's silver and gold mines. The Spanish brought European diseases like smallpox, and epidemics killed many of the natives.

War of Independence and the Mexican-American War

Mexico's war of independence from Spain began in 1810. On September 16, Father Miguel Hidalgo, a small town priest, rang his church bell and shouted "Viva Mexico!" Each September 16, the anniversary of this day, is Mexico's Independence Day.

In 1821, after much fighting, the Empire of Mexico was established. Years of war and unrest followed the declaration of independence. From 1846 to 1848, the United States and Mexico fought a war over Texas. Mexico suffered repeated defeats in battle. These defeats resulted in the loss of Texas, Arizona, and California. This land made up half of Mexico's original territory.

Pyramid of the Sun at Teotihuacán.

A plaza near modern Xochimilco.

Xochimilco — the "Venice of Mexico."

Revolution and Reform

In 1863, Mexico was bankrupt. Mexico agreed in 1864 to be ruled by an Austrian emperor who was backed by France. The Mexican army, however, fought for the nation's freedom. In 1867 they beat the French army. Once again, Mexico was free under President Benito Juárez. Juárez, an Indian, was a just ruler who had been driven out of power by the French. In 1876, shortly after the death of Juárez, Porfirio Díaz seized power and ruled as dictator. He restored Mexico to order and progress, but he denied liberty and land to Indians and the poor. His 34-year rule set the stage for the Mexican Revolution.

The Mexican Revolution

The revolution of 1910 had many heroes and martyrs. Francisco (Panchito) Madero was the first president following the Díaz dictatorship. Pancho Villa was a former bandit and rebel leader in the north. And Emiliano Zapata was a peasant leader from the south. Although these heroes were assassinated, all three survive in stories and songs.

Chaos and coups dominated Mexico until 1917. That was the year a progressive Constitution was set up. This was a major step toward modernization. The revolution cost over a million lives and caused terrible destruction. One out of every eight Mexicans died as a result of the revolution. But it became the basis for Mexican pride and identity as a nation. The revolution meant equal rights and opportunity for all Mexicans. These values are the cornerstone of Mexican government.

Population and Ethnic Groups

The Mexican population (about 80,000,000) is made up of three groups: Indian, 30%; Spanish, 10%; and mixed Indian and Spanish blood, called *mestizo*, 60%. Many of the pureblooded Indians live in mountain regions. There, they keep their traditional languages and customs.

Mexico's population has grown very quickly in recent years. Two sets of numbers show this: 1) Mexico now has 3½ times as many people as in 1940; and 2) three-quarters of all Mexicans are under 30 years old.

Language

Spanish is the national language of Mexico, but over 50 native Indian languages are also still spoken. Spanish is the language of the schools, however. The government's goal is to teach every child to read and write in Spanish.

Religion

More than 95% of Mexicans are Roman Catholic. Catholicism is often mixed with native Indian religions, however, especially for fiestas and for tourists. Unlike many other Christian colonies, Mexico has been tolerant of native beliefs and practices.

Education

Until the revolution, all education was private and the country was largely illiterate. Only the wealthy could attend schools. Mexico now devotes much attention, energy, and money to educating its people. Its literacy rate is now 74%. This means that three out of four adults can read.

Poverty continues to have an effect on Mexican education. Although the government attempts to provide at least ten years of school, many children cannot take advantage of it. Instead, at a very young age they must contribute to the family income. This means that children must learn the skills and handicrafts of their parents. As a result, fewer than 10% of children between 11 and 15 attend school.

One-third of Mexico's budget goes to education. This figure is much higher than in most countries. This may be why the government has so successfully educated its people, despite the rapidly increasing population and variety of complex Indian languages.

Because there are so few teachers, about half the rural schools teach only the first three grades. Some rural schools teach farming techniques to children who will become farmers. Often adults from the area attend to learn more modern ways of farming.

Boys and girls do not attend school together in Mexico. They have separate playgrounds and wings of the school. Sometimes they take part in programs together. Even then, however, they take part in different parts of the program and do not have much contact. They study some of the same things, like Spanish history, arithmetic, and religion. Often, however, the girls study home-related topics like sewing and cooking, while the boys study science and government. These and other courses are designed to prepare boys for further education and careers.

Mexico is home to the oldest university in all the Americas. The National University of Mexico was founded in 1551 in Mexico City. Today it has over 100,000 students. In 1950, the University was expanded and more than 80 new buildings were built. It is now known as University City. During over 300 years of Spanish rule, the university granted 40,000 degrees. But they were granted only to students wealthy enough to attend. Today education is free for all Mexicans, and children study hard in school so a university education can be part of their future.

Art and Music

At the time of the revolution in 1910, three-quarters of Mexican adults could not read. The Ministry of Public Education and Fine Arts hired artists to create art that would educate and inspire the people. José Clemente Orozco, Diego Rivera, and David Alfaro Siqueiros are three great painters. Their art portrays the causes of the Mexican Revolution. Their murals in many public buildings and museums are famous for the way they show Mexican history and culture. Their style is truly Mexican.

Of the three painters, Diego Rivera is perhaps the best known to North Americans. He painted murals in three U.S. cities: Detroit, New York, and San Francisco. His New York mural, in Rockefeller Center, was destroyed, but Rivera later duplicated it in Mexico. In 1940, Rivera painted before large crowds at the Golden Gate International Exposition in San Francisco. The title of this painting is "Pan-American Unity." It shows scenes of ancient Mexican art and modern U.S. technology. It reminds us of the common heritage of Mexico and the western United States.

Music played with European instruments but with Indian and Spanish influences is very popular in Mexico. *Trio, mariachi,* and *marimba* music is often said to express the heart of the Mexican people. A dance called the *Jarabe Tapitio* from the state of Jalisco is the national folkloric dance. Each region of Mexico has music and dances that are special to the people of that region. Mexicans value the variety and liveliness of their folk arts.

Sports

Mexico's most popular sport is soccer, which Mexicans call *fútbol*. In June, 1986, Mexico played host to the World Cup soccer tournament. The major site for the games was Aztec Stadium, which seats 110,000 people. Aztec Stadium is in Mexico City, which sits in a mountain valley 7000 ft (2100 m), or 1⅓ miles (2.1 km), above sea level. People who are not used to such a high altitude often must become used to breathing Mexico City's rather thin — and polluted — air. The air can make playing difficult for many foreign teams.

Also popular in Mexico is *jai-alai*, or *pelota*. This game, which is like handball, comes from the Basque region of Spain. Jai-alai is the fastest ball game in the world. Spain is the source of another popular sport — bullfighting. The Plaza in Mexico City is the world's largest bullring. Other popular sports imports include baseball and basketball from the United States.

Mexicans are known for their excellent horsemanship. They compete in rodeos, known as *charreadas*. Riders wear Mexican *charro* costumes decorated with gold and silver. The famous *sombrero* with its large brim tops off the outfit.

Agriculture

About 33% of the labor force in Mexico is made up of farmers. Their main crops are corn, coffee, sugar cane, cotton, and vegetables. Mexican land is rich, but the rough ground and lack of rainfall make it hard for small landowners to grow their crops. By the year 2000, only about 18% of Mexico's labor force is expected to be made up of farmers.

Under Spanish rule, most of the farming land had been owned by wealthy Spaniards. Indian slaves or peons provided the labor. After the Revolution, the government broke up the haciendas and redistributed the land more fairly.

Today 12% of the land is used for agriculture. The government provides water for much of this land by irrigating it. But because the plots of land are very small, farming is a hard and sometimes unprofitable business. During the winter months, there may be no work at all in the north. This is when thousands of northern farmers leave and work as illegal aliens in the U.S. They return home for the spring and summer to work in the fields. Also, more and more farmers are moving with their families to the cities. There, they join the ranks of the unemployed living in shanty towns.

Times are hard now, but the government is determined to improve farm production. Many programs have been developed that have done much already. Deserts and jungles have been turned into productive farms and ranches. Education programs have helped isolated farms modernize their methods.

Land

The area of Mexico is 761,604 square miles (1,225,421 square km). This area makes Mexico about one-fifth the size of the U.S. Three-quarters of Mexico is a high plateau, between 5000 and 8000 ft (1500 - 2400 m) above sea level. This plateau is between two mountain ranges, the Eastern *(Oriental)* and Western *(Occidental)* Sierra Madres. On the coastal sides of the mountain ranges, rich plains lead to the seas. The land of Mexico varies greatly. It ranges from snowy mountains and volcanoes, to tropical rain forests and deserts. It has shores to the Pacific Ocean, the Caribbean Sea, and the Gulf of Mexico.

Climate

Mexico is divided into five climatic zones — tropical, temperate, cool, plateau, and ice. Along the plains of the seacoast it is possible to swim all year long. Many of the major cities, such as Mexico City and Guadalajara, are in the Central Plateau region in the middle of the country. They have mild weather year-round.

Natural Resources

Mexico is rich in minerals. Long ago, these minerals were exploited by foreign-owned companies. Now Mexicans control each company that mines.

Mexico produces 25% of the world's silver. This makes Mexico the world's largest silver producer. Mexico also has what may well be the world's largest supply of oil reserves. This makes oil Mexico's leading export. Based on its large supply of oil, Mexico borrowed money from international banks. It used this money to develop industry and social programs in the 1970s. The falling prices of oil have now made it hard for Mexico to meet its debts. As profits from the oil industry have gone down, unemployment and poverty have gone up. In addition to oil and silver, Mexico exports copper, gold, lead, zinc, natural gas, and timber to other countries.

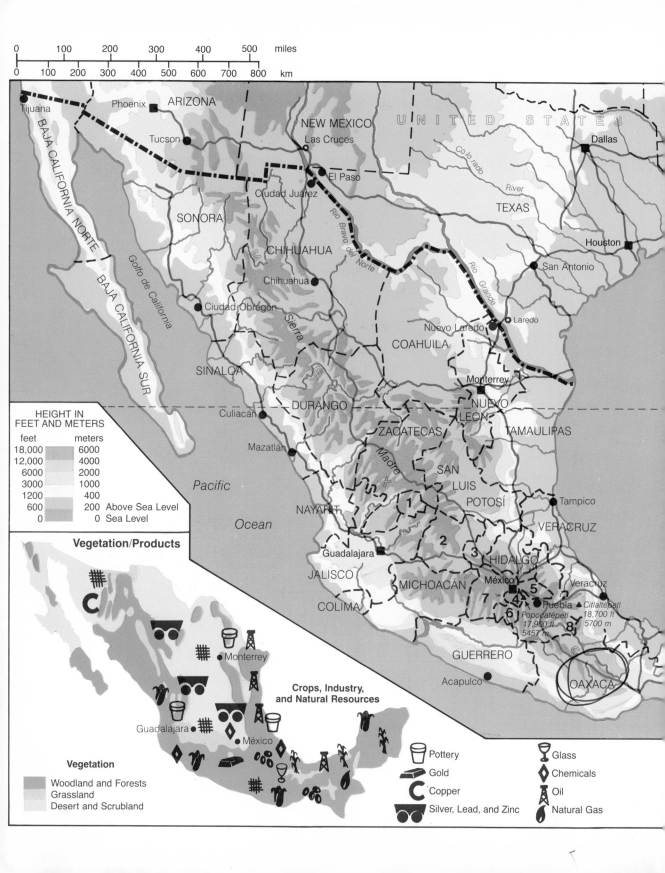

miles
0   100   200   300   400   500

km
0   100   200   300   400   500   600   700   800

Tijuana
Phoenix
ARIZONA
Tucson
NEW MEXICO
Las Cruces
UNITED STATES
Dallas
El Paso
Ciudad Juárez
SONORA
TEXAS
Colorado River
CHIHUAHUA
Houston
Chihuahua
Rio Bravo del Norte
San Antonio
Ciudad Obregón
Rio Grande
BAJA CALIFORNIA NORTE
BAJA CALIFORNIA SUR
Golfo de California
Sierra
Nuevo Laredo
Laredo
COAHUILA
SINALOA
DURANGO
Monterrey
NUEVO LEÓN
TAMAULIPAS
Culiacán
ZACATECAS
Mazatlán
Madre
SAN
LUIS
POTOSÍ
Tampico
Pacific
NAYARIT
VERACRUZ
Ocean
1
2
3
HIDALGO
Guadalajara
México
Veracruz
JALISCO
5
Citlaltépetl
18,700 ft
5700 m
MICHOACÁN
7
4
Puebla
COLIMA
6
Popocatépetl
17,900 ft
5457 m
8
GUERRERO
Acapulco
OAXACA

HEIGHT IN
FEET AND METERS

feet	meters	
18,000	6000	
12,000	4000	
6000	2000	
3000	1000	
1200	400	
600	200	Above Sea Level
0	0	Sea Level

Vegetation/Products

Monterrey
Guadalajara
México

Crops, Industry,
and Natural Resources

Vegetation
Woodland and Forests
Grassland
Desert and Scrubland

Pottery
Gold
Copper
Silver, Lead, and Zinc
Glass
Chemicals
Oil
Natural Gas

MEXICO — Political and Physical

ARKANSAS

MISSISSIPPI

Birmingham

Columbus

GEORGIA

Atlantic
Ocean

Mississippi River

Jackson

ALABAMA

LOUISIANA

Jacksonville

Baton Rouge

New Orleans

FLORIDA

Tampa

THE
BAHAMAS

Gulf
of
Mexico

Miami

Nassau

Tropic of Cancer

Havana

CUBA

Guantánamo

Canal
de
Yucatán

Mérida

YUCATÁN

Golfo
de
Campeche

Caribbean   Sea

JAMAICA

Kingston

QUINTANA
ROO

CAMPECHE

TABASCO

Belize

BELIZE

Golfo de Honduras

CHIAPAS

GUATEMALA

HONDURAS

Tapachula

Guatemala

Tegucigalpa

San
Salvador

EL
SALVADOR

NICARAGUA

Managua

Corn

Coffee

Textiles

Sugar Cane

GENERAL REFERENCE

Countries	States
MEXICO	JALISCO

▬▪▬▪ International Boundaries
- - - - State Boundaries
───── Rivers
───── Major Transportation Routes

States Numbered on Map

1 AGUASCALIENTES	5 TLAXCALA
2 GUANAJUATO	6 MORELOS
3 QUERETARO	7 MÉXICO
4 DISTRITO FEDERAL	8 PUEBLA

■ Guadalajara **Towns over 1,000,000**
● Tijuana **Towns over 100,000**
○ Laredo **Towns under 100,000**

Government

Mexico is a federal republic. It is made up of 31 states and Mexico City, which is a federal district much like Washington, D.C. The president is elected by a direct vote of the citizens for a six-year term. The office of the president is very powerful, but he or she can only be elected to one term. The Congress is made up of two houses. The upper house is called the Chamber of Deputies. It is controlled by the ruling Institutional Revolutionary Party. The lower house, the Senate, has six parties.

A charter member of the United Nations, Mexico takes its role in the world community very seriously. The government takes consistent positions on international issues. It also opposes interference in the problems of other countries. It spends less than 10% of its budget on defense. By comparison, the U.S. spends over 60% on defense.

Mexico is a nonaligned country. This means that it treats international issues on their merits, and not on friendships with other countries. Mexico is unusual in its position among other Latin American countries. It is a post-revolutionary nation. Most of its neighbors, on the other hand, are in pre-revolutionary or revolutionary stages. It opposes all intervention in these countries, either from the United States or from Communist or other Latin American countries. Its votes in the United Nations have reflected these policies.

Currency

The Mexican *peso* and *centavo* are written as $ and ¢. The Mexican peso was once one of the most stable currencies in the world. Now the Mexican economy is very troubled, however, and its currency has lost much of its value.

Mexican currency

Industry

Manufacturing industries have grown rapidly in Mexico. They make up 30% of all Mexican exports. Mexico's exports include crude oil, processed foods, chemicals, basic metals, metal products, rubber, and electric goods.

The factories along the U.S. border are growing rapidly. These factories are known as *maquiladoras*. Here Mexican workers make products from American materials. These products are then sent back to be sold in the U.S. Eighteen percent of the Mexican labor force works in manufacturing.

Non-manufacturing industry includes Mexico's large tourism industry. Tourism provides jobs for many Mexicans, especially in the winter months.

Mexico City

Till 1325 the Aztecs had been a nomadic people. They then discovered the place promised them by their sun god, Huitzilopochtli: "The land where an eagle perches on cactus leaves and holds a serpent in its beak is the land of prosperity." An eagle holding a serpent in its beak: This is the central design of the Mexican flag.

The Aztecs built their capital on this land. They named it Tenochtitlán, which means "alongside the cactus." Spanish colonists later changed the name to Mexico City.

The metropolitan population of Mexico City is around 18 million. This means that Mexico City is today the world's second largest city. Thousands of Indians and mestizos arrive every day to live in the city, and the population grows by over 600,000 people a year. One sign of Mexico City's rapid growth is poverty and overcrowded living conditions. Mexico City has around five hundred slums. They are called *ciudades perdidas*, or lost cities. By the year 2000, experts predict that the population will be over 30 million.

Alongside the old buildings and the old culture are modern buildings, highways, and subways. Mexico City's traffic jams, pollution, and housing problems are matched by few cities anywhere. In many ways, however, its relaxed Latin pace of life still survives.

The center of the city is a large square. Its official name is *Plaza de la Constitución* (Constitution Plaza); but it is known to everyone as the *Zócalo*. Here, at the National Palace, the president of Mexico strikes the bell at 11 p.m. on September 15 every year. He is joined by the crowds in the Zócalo shouting "Viva Mexico!" This begins the celebration of Mexico's independence from Spain.

A busy plaza near a train station in Mexico City.

Inside and around Mexico City the ancient culture of Mexico is seen in Aztec ruins and in museums, churches, and palaces. And yet the city is full of new things, such as the Latin American Tower. The tallest building in Mexico, it was designed by American architect Frank Lloyd Wright. Its foundation is made of floating chambers.

These chambers have helped the Latin American Tower resist Mexico City's frequent floods and earthquakes. Many other modern buildings in Mexico City were not so well-designed. They were among the hundreds of buildings destroyed in the earthquakes of 1985.

Mexico City: a modern metropolis sitting in a mountain valley, 7000 feet above sea level.

The Plaza of the Three Cultures is symbolic of present-day Mexico. Here are remains of Aztec temples and pyramids, Santiago Church from the colonial period, and ultramodern contemporary buildings. At one glance, visitors can see three periods of architectural style.

The subway, built jointly by the French and Mexican governments.

Another symbol of both the present and the past in Mexico City is the subway system. Each station has its own symbol for those who can't read. While building the Pino Suárez station, workers discovered the remains of an Aztec temple. Now the station is a museum as well as a subway stop. The bright orange cars ride on rubber covered wheels. This makes them so quiet that music is piped into the stations.

58

Two earthquakes struck Mexico City on September 19th and 20th in 1985. These quakes did huge damage to a city where many people already lived in shanty towns and tents. In just two days, two large hospitals and four hundred office buildings were destroyed. Two hundred schools were damaged or destroyed. In all, more than eleven hundred buildings were badly damaged or destroyed. More than 31,000 people were left without homes. Within hours of the first quake, trained rescue teams from all over the world arrived in Mexico City to help search for survivors.

The patience and courage of the people of Mexico City provided moments of joy in the days following the tragedy. Eight days after the quakes, a newborn baby was found alive in the ruins of a hospital, and the whole world rejoiced.

Mexicans North of the Border

Do you know that one-quarter of the United States was once Mexico? In 1848 Mexico lost half of its land in the Mexican-American War.

Today, around eleven million people of Mexican descent are citizens of the United States. In addition, an estimated six million live and work in the U.S. illegally. Though many live in poverty, over two thousand Mexican-Americans hold elected offices. Because jobs are so few and wages are so low in Mexico, many people come to the U.S. to work at jobs that most Americans do not want.

Along the U.S.-Mexican border an industry has grown up. Materials are sent from the U.S. side to the factories known as *maquiladoras* on the Mexican side. There the materials are made into products by Mexicans who work for lower wages than Americans would. The products are then sent back to the United States to be sold. By 1990 the maquiladoras will employ over a million people. Today the maquiladora program is second only to oil as a source of U.S. dollars in Mexico.

Compared to the millions of Mexicans and Mexican-Americans living in the U.S., only several thousand reside in Canada. Despite small numbers and great distances, however, Mexicans do work in Canada. Mexicans who want to work in Canada must go through a process that is far more formal and complicated than in the U.S. Both the Mexican and Canadian governments review the applications of people wishing to work in Canada. This process can be long and complicated.

Glossary of Useful Mexican Terms

adios (ah-DYOS) . . . . good-bye
bebeleche (beh-beh-LAY-cheh) . . . . a hopscotch game
beisbol (BAZE-bol) . . . . baseball
carne (CAR-nay) . . . . meat
centavo (sen-TAH-boh) . . . . cent
charreada (char-ray-AH-dah) . . . . rodeo

charro (CHAR-oh)	a Mexican horseman who wears a special costume
chili (CHEE-lay)	hot pepper
ciudad (syu-DAD)	city (plural ciudades [syu-DAD-es])
corrido (cor-REE-doh)	ballad; a song that tells a story
domingo (doh-MEEN-goh)	Sunday
fiesta (fee-ES-tah)	a festival or holiday
fútbol (FOOT-bol)	soccer, Mexico's most popular sport
hacienda (ah-see-EN-dah)	large farm or estate
¡hasta la vista! (AH-stah lah BEE-stah)	good-bye!
jai-alai (HI-ah-li)	a game played against a tall wall with a ball and hand-held basket
jugo (HU-goh)	juice
libertad (lee-ber-TAD)	liberty
mariachi (mah-ree-AH-chee)	Mexican music and band typical of Guadalajara
matador (mah-tah-DOR)	bullfighter who kills the bull
mejicano (meh-hee-CAHN-oh)	Mexican
mestizos (mes-TEE-zos)	people of mixed Spanish and Indian background
mi (mee)	my
muchas gracias (MU-chas GRAH-sias)	thank you very much
no (no)	no
número (NU-meh-roh)	number
pelota (peh-LOH-tah)	the game of jai-alai; also, the ball used in jai-alai
perdido (pare-DEE-doh)	lost
peso (PEH-soh)	unit of currency in some countries
pichón (peeh-SHONE)	pigeon
piñata (peen-YAH-tah)	hanging pot filled with treats
pueblo (PWEH-bloh)	village
rey (rray)	king (plural reyes [RRAY-es])
rosca (RROSE-kah)	crown-shaped roll; circle
sangre (SAN-gray)	blood
sí (see)	yes
siesta (see-ES-tah)	afternoon nap
sombrero (som-BRER-oh)	hat
submarino (sube-mah-REE-noh)	submarine
taco (TAH-coh)	a folded tortilla sandwich
toreo (toh-RAY-oh)	bullfighting
torero (toh-RARE-oh)	bullfighter
toro (TOH-roh)	bull
tortilla (tor-TEE-ah)	a thin, toasted cake of cornmeal
tostada (tohs-TAH-dah)	a kind of tortilla
zócalo (ZOH-cah-loh)	public square

More Books About Mexico

Listed below are more books about Mexico. If you are interested in them, check your library. You may find many of them helpful in doing research for some of the "Things to Do" projects that follow.

Ancient America. Greenhaven Press Editors (Greenhaven)
Aztecs. Crosher (Macdonald)
Cooking the Mexican Way. Coronado (Lerner)
Family in Mexico. Jacobsen (Bookwright)
The Hispanic Americans. Meltzer (Harper & Row)
Hungry Woman: Myths and Legends of the Aztecs. (Morrow)
Indian Arts, North America. Whiteford (Putnam)
Mexican Revolution. Greenhaven Press Editors (Greenhaven)
Mexicans in America. Pinchot (Greenhaven)
Mexico, Giant of the South. Smith (Dillon)
The Picture Story of Nancy Lopez. Phillips (Messner)
Why Corn Is Golden. Blackmore (Little Brown)

Things to Do — Research Projects

Governments and economies change quickly. In the mid 1970s, for example, the future looked very bright for Mexico because of its large supply of oil. In less than ten years, however, the world's demand for oil had diminished. Mexico was unable to sell its oil at the high prices it needed to continue the projects it had begun. Since 1982, the standard of living in Mexico has dropped 40%.

As you read about Mexico or any country, keep in mind the importance of having current information. Some of the research projects that follow need accurate, up-to-date information. That is why current newspapers and magazines are useful sources of information. Two publications your library may have will tell you about recent magazine and newspaper articles on many topics:

The Reader's Guide to Periodical Literature
Children's Magazine Guide

For accurate answers to questions about such topics of current interest as Mexico's earthquakes, economy, oil industry, and social and educational progress, look up *Mexico* in these two publications. They will lead you to the most up-to-date information you can find.

1. Some of the early Indian people of Mexico, such as the Toltecs, the Maya, and the Aztecs, developed great civilizations and became very powerful. Pick one of these peoples and do further research to learn more about their contributions to art, architecture, and science.
2. Draw two pictures that compare the architecture in two different ancient or modern Mexican civilizations.
3. How far is Guadalajara from where you live? Use maps, travel guides, travel agents, or any other resources you know of. Find out how you could get there and how long it would take.
4. Many rural Mexicans have moved to the cities in search of work and new opportunities. Thousands of mestizos and Indians come to Mexico City every day. Some have found prosperity. More have found worse poverty than they left.

Find the answers to these questions: Why have people moved to the cities? What must the cities have for this kind of movement to succeed? How does this situation compare with movement, or migration, in your country?

5. Write a short report about a resource or industry important to the Mexican economy. Be sure your information is current, at least within the last year.

6. Imagine that your parents decide to move to Mexico. They ask you which area you would like to live in. Investigate further about Mexico and pick a location. Give your reasons.

7. Pick a Mexican holiday that your country also celebrates. How do the two celebrations resemble each other? How are they different?

8. Look up Mexico in the *Reader's Guide to Periodical Literature* or the *Children's Magazine Guide*. Find articles that have been written recently, and report to your classmates about what has been happening in the last few months.

More Things to Do — Activities

These projects are designed to encourage further thinking and talking about Mexico. They offer ideas and suggestions for interesting group or individual projects that you can do at school or at home.

1. Invite somebody from Mexico to visit your class to talk about his or her country. Prepare a list of interesting questions to ask.

2. How does your life compare with Elena's? Write a paragraph describing the ways in which you are the same or different.

3. If you were going to talk to a child from Mexico, what questions would you ask?

4. See if your class or another group you belong to wants to have a Mexican fiesta. You might want to have one for a birthday party. Decide what Mexican food you want to serve and dress in Mexican-style clothing. Your fiesta will look more like a real Mexican fiesta if you decorate the room.

5. If you would like a pen pal in Mexico, write to these people:

International Pen Friends
P.O. Box 65
Brooklyn, New York 11229

Be sure to tell them what country you want your pen pal to be from. Also, include your full name and address.

Index